Painting

Sea Life

in Oil

Mia Tavonatti

Walter Foster

Tools & Materials

Good-quality art materials are important for successful painting results. Always buy the best materials you can afford, especially when it comes to paints and brushes.

Damar Varnish   Squeeze Bottle   Turpentine   Linseed Oil

My Work Station

Painting Medium

Painting medium is used to thin the oil paints. For the transparent glazes used in this book, prepare a mixture of 1/5 damar varnish, 1/5 linseed oil, and 3/5 turpentine. Mix the medium in a clear squeeze bottle that has measurement marks and a small tip so you can control how much medium you add to the paints.

Mahlstick

Workable Fixative

A workable fixative (not shown) should be used to set your drawing after you transfer it to the painting surface. This will keep the drawing from dissolving when you apply paint.

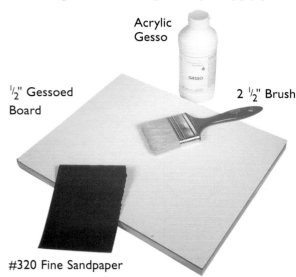

Acrylic Gesso

1/2" Gessoed Board

2 1/2" Brush

#320 Fine Sandpaper

Work Station

It is important to have an organized work station, where all your supplies are within close reach. Make sure your station is in a well-ventilated area with a good light source—natural or halogen lighting is best.

Easel

Several types of easels are available. A vertical tabletop easel is a good choice, and the table provides space for your supplies. You can tape your reference images to the easel for easy referral.

Palette

Disposable paper palettes are convenient because you can just tear the top page off when it gets too full of paint. This helps you avoid "muddy colors" that result from an overused palette.

Always clean your brushes with soap and water at the end of the painting session.

Mahlstick

A mahlstick is a tool on which you rest your hand to keep it steady for accurate detail work. You can use a long stick of smooth wood or a wooden dowel, whichever is more comfortable for you.

Brush Cleaning Jar

Keep a brush cleaning jar filled with colorless mineral spirits or turpentine within easy reach. Jars with a wire coil near the bottom trap the paint sediments that sink to the bottom, which helps keep the thinner clean.

Brushes

Bristle brushes normally used for oil painting aren't suitable for the kind of detail work demonstrated in this book because the hairs are too stiff; use soft-bristled sable brushes instead. White "nylon sable" brushes aren't as expensive as real sable, and they work just as well.

Painting Surfaces

You will want a smooth painting surface for this translucent style of painting. Gesso panels are a good choice. They're available at art supply stores, or you can prepare them yourself by applying one or two layers of acrylic gesso to a hardboard panel. With each layer, alternate the direction of your strokes and gently sand the surface. The end result should be a fine, smooth surface, similar to that of an eggshell.

2 1/2" Brush

Very Fine Round   Fine Round   Medium Round   Fan   Small Palette Knife   1/2" Flat   1/4" Flat   1/8" Flat

Oil Paints

Below is the selection of oil colors that are used most often for the paintings in this book. This palette can be expanded by mixing some of the colors together as shown in the color mixing charts below. It is important to note that colors with more white in them, such as cerulean blue, are more opaque than colors without white, such as phthalo blue, alizarin crimson, and sap green.

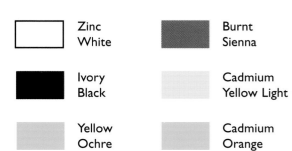

Zinc White

Ivory Black

Yellow Ochre

Burnt Sienna

Cadmium Yellow Light

Cadmium Orange

Cadmium Red Light

Alizarin Crimson

Cobalt Violet

Sap Green

Green-Gold Hue

Phthalo Yellow-Green

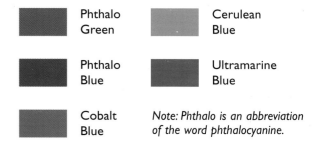

Phthalo Green

Phthalo Blue

Cobalt Blue

Cerulean Blue

Ultramarine Blue

Note: Phthalo is an abbreviation of the word phthalocyanine.

Color Mixing

Two or more paint colors can be combined to create a new color, or one color can be used to warm, cool, or gray another color. *Warm* colors are those that have more red in them; *cool* colors are those that have more blue; and a *grayed* color is one that is more neutral. Note, however, that warm colors aren't just yellows, oranges, and reds, and cool colors aren't just blues, greens, and purples. Some blues are warmer than other blues, and some reds are cooler than other reds. For example, cerulean blue is warmer than ultramarine blue, and alizarin crimson is cooler than cadmium red.

Water Temperature and Depth Color

Near the surface, the water appears warmer and lighter than it does near the bottom. Refer to the chart below when painting different water depths.

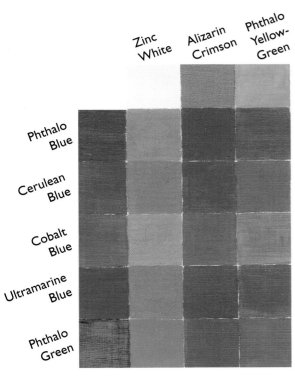

Cool Colors

In the example above, different cool colors were achieved by adding one of the colors at the top (the columns) with each of the colors at the left (the rows). For example, the color below zinc white is a combination of zinc white and phthalo blue; the next color in that row is a combination of alizarin crimson and phthalo blue; the color below that is a combination of alizarin crimson and cerulean blue; and so on. (A little zinc white was added to each to better show the colors.)

Try to match the colors shown here by experimenting with varying amounts of the different colors.

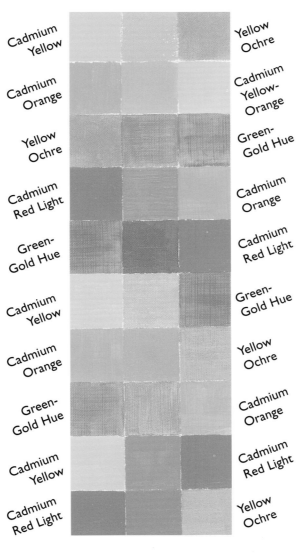

Warm Colors

In the example above, the warm colors in the middle column are achieved by mixing equal amounts of the color on the left and the color on the right. Notice that all of these warms are created by mixing only five different colors in various combinations.

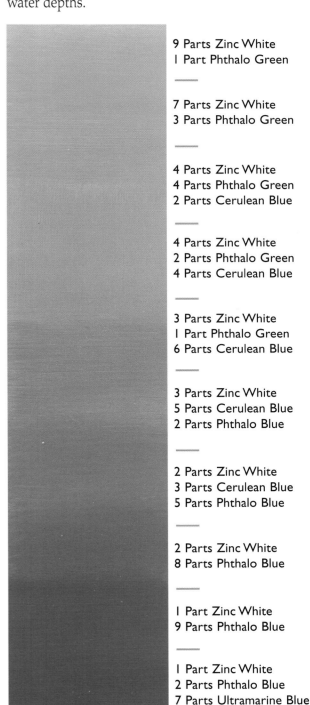

9 Parts Zinc White
1 Part Phthalo Green

7 Parts Zinc White
3 Parts Phthalo Green

4 Parts Zinc White
4 Parts Phthalo Green
2 Parts Cerulean Blue

4 Parts Zinc White
2 Parts Phthalo Green
4 Parts Cerulean Blue

3 Parts Zinc White
1 Part Phthalo Green
6 Parts Cerulean Blue

3 Parts Zinc White
5 Parts Cerulean Blue
2 Parts Phthalo Blue

2 Parts Zinc White
3 Parts Cerulean Blue
5 Parts Phthalo Blue

2 Parts Zinc White
8 Parts Phthalo Blue

1 Part Zinc White
9 Parts Phthalo Blue

1 Part Zinc White
2 Parts Phthalo Blue
7 Parts Ultramarine Blue

Composition & Perspective

Composition and perspective are two important things to keep in mind when planning a painting. Composition is simply the organization and arrangement of the elements in a painting (or drawing), and the rules of perspective allow you to depict three-dimensional objects on a flat surface, giving the illusion of depth and distance.

Arranging the Elements

The key to capturing the sense of mystery, strength, and otherworldliness in marine paintings is to create compositions that put the viewer in the middle of the action. An effective composition has a sense of balance and leads the viewer's eye to the focal point, or interest area. When depicting sea life, it is important to create a sense of movement. Circular compositions (near right) are good for creating movement and rhythm because the eye is directed along a visual path from object to object. The viewer's focus is always kept at the center of the picture, instead of trailing off of the composition into the unknown.

Creating the Illusion of Depth

You will need a general knowledge of perspective to add realism and dimension to your paintings. Simply put, the closer to the viewer an object is, the larger it should appear, and the farther away it is, the smaller it should appear. Vary the sizes of objects in the foreground, middle ground, and background to show that they are not all on the same plane. This is known as the *depth of field.*

Circular Composition
Arrange the elements in a circular pattern to draw the viewer's eye to the center of the painting.

Notice how the jellyfish in the composition below (left) overlap all four sides of the picture plane. This gives the viewer a feeling of being inside the picture. So does varying the viewing angle—another element of perspective. Because some of the jellyfish are viewed from below and others from above, they appear to surround the viewer, floating up and away.

Triangular compositions (below) are a traditional form of organizing objects in a painting. This was the type of composition often used by the old masters. Triangular compositions make use of diagonals to create balanced layouts that always lead the eye back to center.

Triangular or Pyramidal Composition
Organize the elements in a triangular pattern to lead the eye along diagonal lines toward the focal point.

A sense of depth can also be enhanced by adding atmospheric effects, a technique referred to as *atmospheric perspective* (also called *aerial perspective*). Atmospheric perspective shows how moisture and particles in the air soften and cool images over distance. Atmospheric effects are achieved by varying the values, by using both warm and cool colors, and by contrasting sharply focused imagery in the foreground with softer, more painterly imagery in the background. The sea lion painting at the left is an excellent example of the use of atmosphere perspective, which is particularly evident in the kelp. Notice how the use of this technique increases the sense of depth, and how the triangular composition leads the eye up, toward the buoy.

Depth of Field
Use perspective techniques to create the illusion of a foreground, middle ground, and background on a flat painting surface.

Atmospheric Perspective
For images in the foreground, use dense, warm colors and crisp, sharp details; for images in the background, use paler, cooler colors and softer, fewer details.

Evolution of a Drawing

The first step in composing a painting is to make a pencil drawing of the subject. This way, you can work out the composition, perspective, and all the other details before applying any color to your painting surface.

Thumbnails

Start the drawing by doing several thumbnails. *Thumbnails* are small-scale sketches used for working out the composition. By working small, you can focus on the rhythm or motion of the composition and on the general massing of the subjects—that is, how much space they take up.

Thumbnails

Drawing Studies

Drawing Studies

Using reference photos as models (see box at right), practice drawing each subject individually. Study the photos to see how the subject really looks—not how you think it should look. After doing several studies of the subjects, you will be able to render them accurately in your final drawing.

Final Drawing

Begin the final drawing by enlarging the thumbnail on a photocopy machine. Then place a piece of tracing paper over the copy and start refining the lines. You may have to do two or three such drawings, with each more accurate and detailed than the previous one, to arrive at a final version. Once the drawing is complete, you can transfer it to the final painting surface using artist's carbon paper. Then spray it with a couple of light coats of workable fixative so the lines don't dissolve when you apply paint.

Final Drawing

COLLECTING AND USING REFERENCES

Assembling accurate, clear, and detailed references, or models, is essential. Take photographs, and collect images from magazines and books. Find photos that show sea life subjects in a variety of activities. Also look for materials that show the color and lighting effects you'd like to replicate. Remember, reference material is just a source of information. You should use elements from different references, rearrange the composition, vary the colors, and add your own touches to create an original painting.

Lighting and Color Sample

Subjects in Motion

Detail Shot

5

The Stages of a Painting

It takes many thin layers of paint to create a sea life painting that has depth and a sense of light. By starting with a transparent underpainting and using a variety of glazing and drybrushing layers to slowly build the elements, you will arrive at a more interesting and varied finished product. For the paintings in this book, follow the seven basic steps below. (Note: Start at the bottom of the page and work your way up.)

 ### Final Lighting

Finally, apply several layers of paint to build up the bright whites. Make sure you let each layer dry before applying another. Then step back and evaluate your painting, looking for any last-minute details that need to be added.

 ### Drybrushing Highlights

Allow the painting to dry before applying these layers. Use very opaque colors mixed with zinc white (with no medium added) to brighten the light areas and apply highlights. Hold your 1/8" or 1/4" brush very softly on its flat side, and gently lay on the paint in a downward stroke so it can pick up the slight texture of the board. This will keep the color bright and opaque while allowing the colors underneath to show through, as in the example at the right.

 White Drybrush over Phthalo Blue Glaze

 ### Second Glazing

After the opaque colors are dry, deepen the shadows and enliven any flat areas by adding more layers of glaze. Any colors, such as phthalo blue, ultramarine blue, and sap green will work when thinned with painting medium. Study the glaze sample at the right to see how to build up the depth of color.

 Phthalo Blue Glaze

 ### Blending Opaque Layer

Softly blend the opaque colors with a completely dry, very soft brush to achieve a smooth transition between the colors. Use short, gentle strokes (barely touching the surface) to smooth out the earlier brush strokes. Long strokes will run all the colors together and result in dirty or muddy colors. For the shadows, carefully blend in paint from the light areas so the paint graduates from opaque light to transparent shadows.

 ### Opaque Layer

In the areas that are hit by light, start to lay in small patches of opaque color (cool reds, sap greens, and blues mixed with small amounts of white) in short vertical strokes using a 1/4" flat brush. Work on one area at a time because you will have to blend the paint before it dries to achieve a smooth finish. Don't blend these areas together yet, but apply enough paint to cover the underpainting. (At this point, it should look very much like an impressionist painting.) Later you will gradually blend the color into the shadow and detail areas.

 ### Glazing Shadows

Using thin, transparent layers of color mixed with painting medium, start to darken the shadow areas. (Here, phthalo blue was used.) Soften the edges of the glazed strokes with a soft, dry brush until they blend smoothly with the surrounding area. Let each layer dry before adding another, or you will start to pick up the color underneath.

Underpainting

Using a 1/2" flat brush, apply an even layer of thin, transparent color for the background and shadow color. (Here, phthalo blue was mixed with plenty of painting medium to create a very translucent color.) Pat this layer with a clean soft cloth rolled into a ball to even out the color and remove excess paint so you can clearly see your drawing through the paint. Use a rag or cotton swabs to gently remove color where the light hits the subject.

Water Effects

Painting water can be challenging because it takes on so many different qualities. Various things can affect the appearance of water—for example, the wind, the tide, the depth, the distance from the shore, and the light. It can be still one minute and churning the next; it can appear clear, blue, green, or even black. As you practice these painting techniques, keep checking your reference photos to accurately replicate the different water qualities.

Light Filtering in Through Water

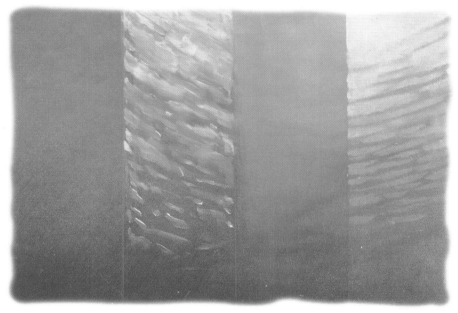

➡ Begin with a transparent base glaze in gradations, from phthalo green at the surface to phthalo blue at the bottom, and blend lightly with a dry brush.

➡ Add patches of opaque zinc white, using more at the surface, where the light is strongest. Allow more of the base glaze to show through at the bottom.

➡ Thoroughly blend in the patches of white with a dry, soft brush. Try to create a very smooth gradation from light to dark.

➡ When the paint has dried, add more patches of strong zinc white, and soften them slightly with a dry brush.

Water Surface Reflections

Start at the bottom and work up.

⬆ Finally, using a wide, very soft, and completely dry brush, blend the paint, stroking from left to right very lightly so you don't smear or spread the paint.

⬆ Now add the white highlights on the ripples with generous amounts of opaque zinc white.

⬆ Then begin spontaneously painting in irregular, horizontal patterns with deep phthalo blue, and a small, fine round brush.

⬆ First apply a transparent layer of phthalo blue.

Light Reflections Underwater

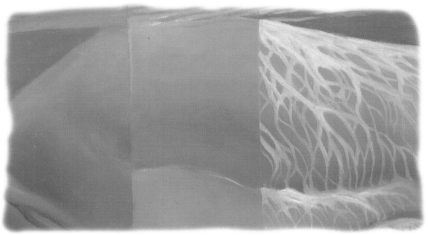

➡ Lay in the basic underpainting with semiopaque phthalo green and ultramarine blue mixed with small amounts of white.

➡ Drybrush in light areas with opaque white mixed with phthalo green.

➡ Use the point of a fine round brush to add highlights of opaque white, and soften these edges with a dry, soft brush.

Above and Below the Water's Surface

Sky

Water Surface

Below Surface

➡ First lay in an underpainting of phthalo blue mixed with medium, using variations of lighter and darker blue on the horizon line. Blend with a soft brush.

➡ Then apply opaque zinc white just below the surface line, and blend it down into the blue with a dry, soft brush or your finger.

➡ After the paint has dried, punch up the lighting with more opaque white, and use a blending brush to soften the edges.

Shore Elements

For this kind of painting, success really lies in attention to details. These two pages contain several elements that can add to the interest of your paintings. Each element is shown at various stages of development, from the initial underpainting through the final drybrushed detail. Use the same painting techniques that were explained on pages 6 and 7.

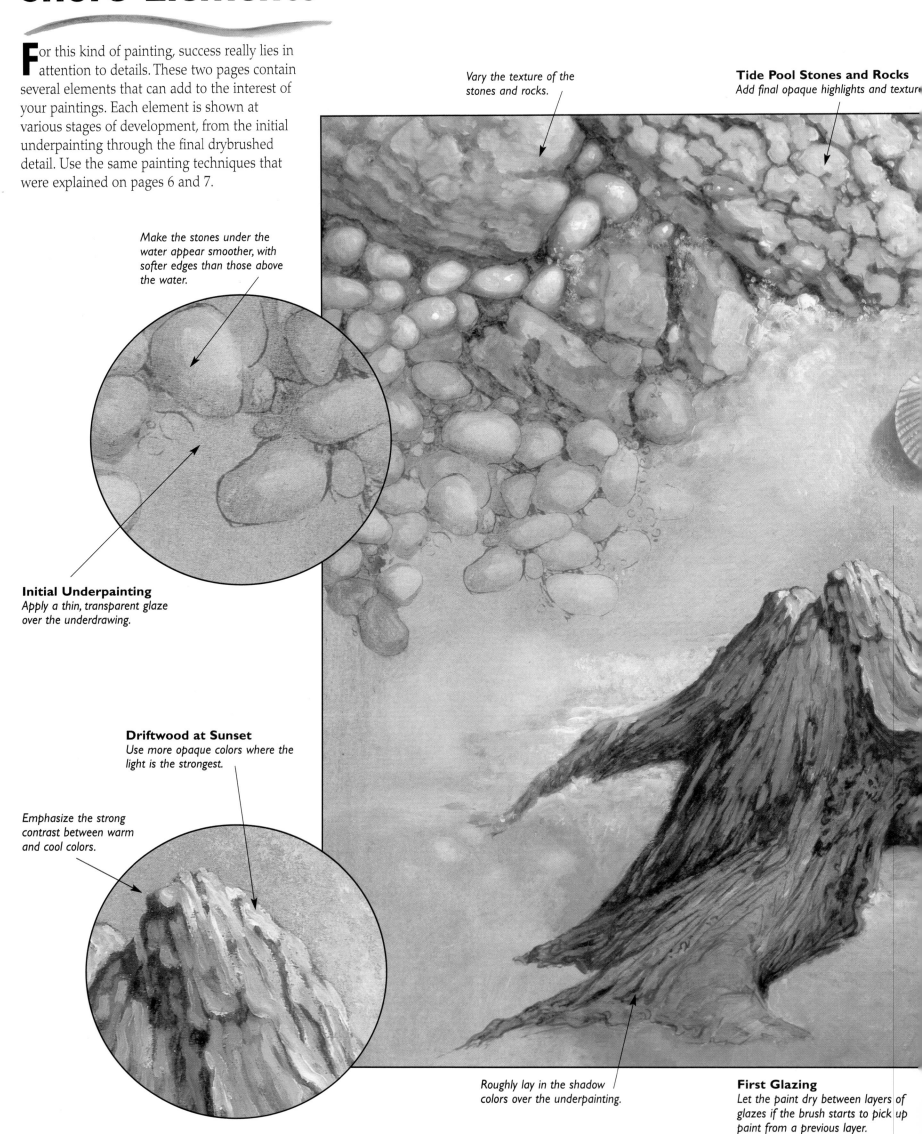

Make the stones under the water appear smoother, with softer edges than those above the water.

Initial Underpainting
Apply a thin, transparent glaze over the underdrawing.

Driftwood at Sunset
Use more opaque colors where the light is the strongest.

Emphasize the strong contrast between warm and cool colors.

Vary the texture of the stones and rocks.

Tide Pool Stones and Rocks
Add final opaque highlights and texture

Roughly lay in the shadow colors over the underpainting.

First Glazing
Let the paint dry between layers of glazes if the brush starts to pick up paint from a previous layer.

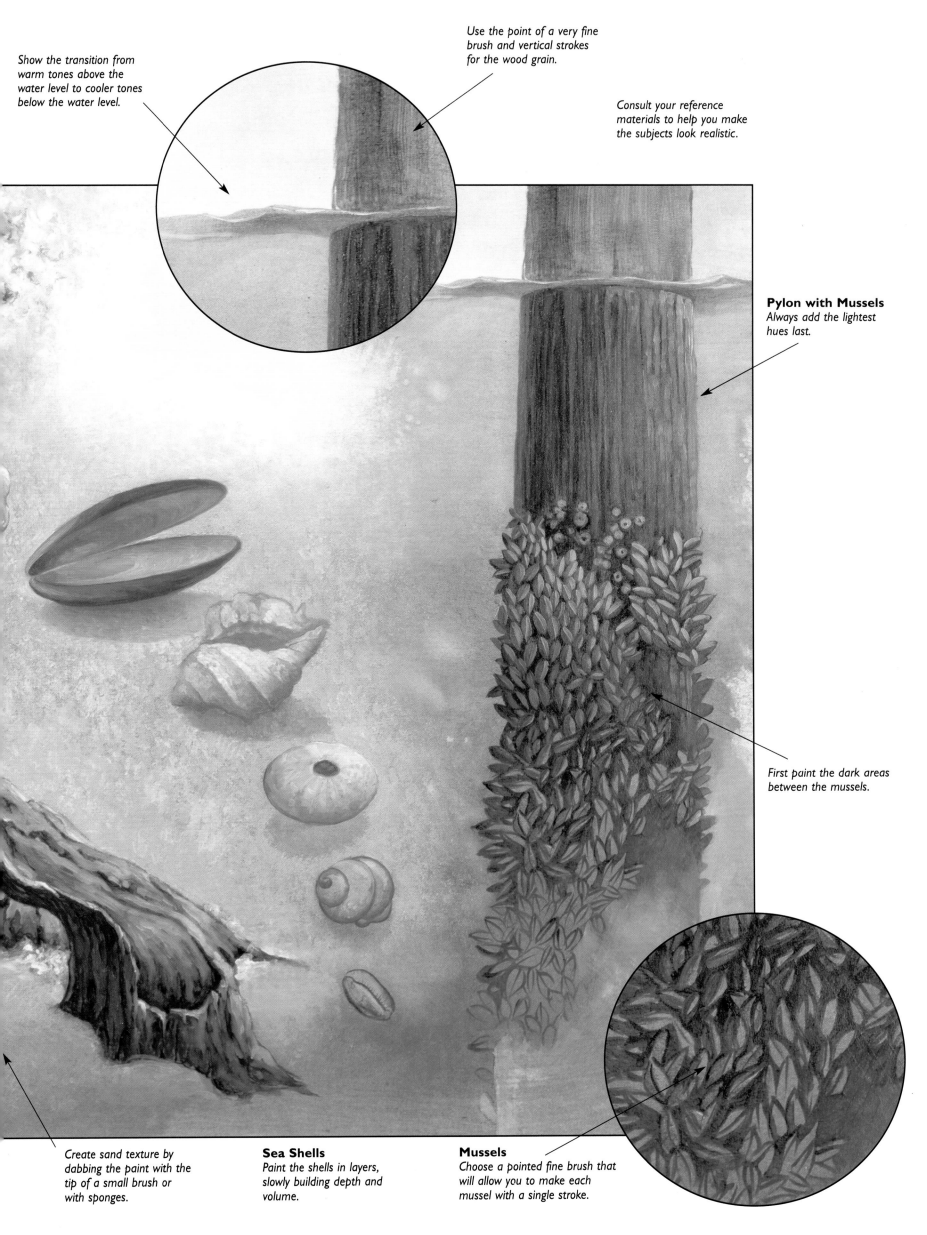

Show the transition from warm tones above the water level to cooler tones below the water level.

Use the point of a very fine brush and vertical strokes for the wood grain.

Consult your reference materials to help you make the subjects look realistic.

Pylon with Mussels
Always add the lightest hues last.

First paint the dark areas between the mussels.

Create sand texture by dabbing the paint with the tip of a small brush or with sponges.

Sea Shells
Paint the shells in layers, slowly building depth and volume.

Mussels
Choose a pointed fine brush that will allow you to make each mussel with a single stroke.

Flora & Fauna

No matter what the specific subject, all these forms of sea life are painted by following the same process. Each one starts with an underpainting, is built up with glazes and opaque layers, and then is finished with highlights, as explained step by step on page 6.

Giant Green Anemone
Use the side of a pointed fine round brush to softly apply the final details.

Brain Sponge
To create the crease areas and add volume, use a glaze of the same color as the underpainting, only darker.

Plate Coral

When creating depth, remember that, generally, warm colors come forward, so they are used in the foreground; cool colors are used for areas that recede.

Sea Fan
Paint around the negative space of the background.

Sea Anemone
When everything is dry, paint the lightest areas.

Kelp
To achieve this transparent look, let the darker shadow areas of the background leaves show through the foreground leaves.

The kelp is lightest and most transparent near the top.

Sea Sponge
Pay attention to size relationships, so that all the elements stay in proper proportion.

Sea Urchin

Be careful to retain some transparency when applying the kelp's underpainting.

Add final highlights with opaque paint.

Dolphins at Play

Now that you have learned to create dynamic compositions, have mastered the seven basic steps for building a painting with depth, and have gained some experience in mixing warm and cool colors, it's time to move on to the complete painting. (Refer to page 6 as needed for basic information on building depth.)

Remember, it is important to work out all the details in your final drawing. You don't want to have to make changes on the painting surface. Many of your paintings will be very transparent overall, and any extraneous pencil marks may show through.

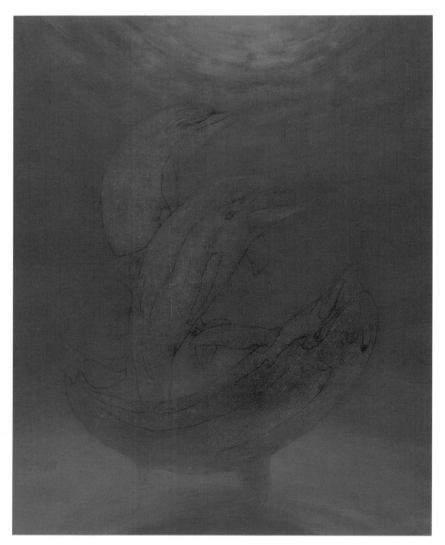

Transfer the final drawing to the painting surface with artist's carbon paper and lightly spray with workable fixative. Then use a 1/2" flat brush to apply a very transparent glaze of phthalo blue at the top and center for the water, and a glaze of phthalo green at the bottom to suggest the lighter sandy floor (above left). Use white and a fine round brush to create the patterns of light filtering through the water's surface. Then smooth the gradations of color by lightly blending with a very soft, very dry, large flat brush.

With a pointed fine round brush, lay in some darker phthalo blue glazes in the shadow areas. Add light values of white mixed with a little blue on the dolphins' underbellies and for highlighted areas. Use more opaque white at the top where the light is coming through the water, and blend this area softly to create vertical light rays (above).

To finish the painting, punch up the forms by deepening the darkest areas with another glaze layer and by brightening the highlights with a clean white. Use the side of a flat brush to pick up the texture of the board.

Continue to build dark shadow areas on the dolphins using additional glaze layers, and then add white highlights. As a final touch, add white bubbles in varying sizes to give depth to the painting.

Mother & Baby Whales

The aim of this composition is both to create a feeling of intimacy between the mother and baby and to convey the sense of a whale's strength and power. Using the whole space available suggests intimacy, and the dramatic angle of the animals and their wakes makes a very powerful composition, with a strong sense of motion as well.

Gradually add glazes of deeper phthalo blue to enhance the volume and light effects (above). Use warm phthalo blue-whites near the surface and cool ultramarine blues for the deeper water.

First transfer the final drawing to the board and spray with workable fixative. Then apply an underpainting of transparent phthalo blue. Next, consider the light source as you establish the light areas and the shadows by removing some of the paint with a soft cloth (above).

Now the whales' forms begin to take shape. After building up the darks, start creating general volume by adding lighter values of opaque phthalo blue mixed with varying amounts of white. Then develop the wave action with various mixes of opaque phthalo green and white.

For the finishing touches, bring up the lights by adding some strong, opaque whites, especially at the water's surface and in the wakes. Then add some light patterns on the whales' backs with a pointed fine round brush. (Check your reference photos often.) Finally, clean up the dark lines around the eyes and mouths with the point of a fine round brush and dark transparent phthalo blue.

Hammerhead Sharks

This composition of a pack of hammerhead sharks makes use of atmospheric perspective (see page 4). That is, you create depth by depicting sharks at varying levels of detail, reserving the greatest detail and strongest highlights for the largest shark in the foreground. Allow some of the sharks to swim out of sight, and vary the viewing angle to increase the drama of the composition.

Next add layers of opaque paint in the water and on the sharks to smooth out the texture (above). Blend the paint more on the background sharks, where soft, hazy edges increase the sense of depth.

Transfer the drawing, and apply a thin underpainting of phthalo blue (above). Then develop the dark areas with warm phthalo blue glazes on the sharks in front, cool ultramarine blue glazes on the sharks in back, and phthalo green and sap green glazes on the vegetation.

Continue adding color to the coral using very cool tones of phthalo green mixed with white and various reds. Also keep building the volume of the sharks by adding more layers of brighter blues and white (above).

In the final stage, punch up all the color, especially on the coral and the shark in the foreground. Add pure whites on the largest shark, and sharpen the details using a fine brush. Then brighten the highlights at the water's surface with pure white.

Ocean Floor with Octopus & Eel

Octopuses and eels are often found hiding in dark, secluded places. This triangular composition incorporates a deep, dark sea cave with light filtering in from outside and above. Remember that triangular compositions use diagonal lines to direct the viewer's eye toward the focal point—the octopus, in this case. Contrasts of light and dark also help create interest and drama.

Create texture in the octopus by stippling the paint on with the tip of an old, worn, and flattened brush.

For the underpainting (above), use phthalo green to show warmth where the light comes in from above; use the cooler phthalo blue for the rocks and cave. Make a transparent purple with ultramarine blue, alizarin crimson, and painting medium for the octopus and ocean floor.

Using a small flat brush, increase the darkness of the cave and crevices (above) with layers of deep, transparent phthalo blue, adding some sap green in the darkest areas. Then add cool alizarin crimson or Indian red with white and violets for the octopus, and sap green and phthalo green for the eel.

The most important part of this painting is to make sure the octopus doesn't look like a cutout pasted onto a background. To avoid this problem, be sure to integrate the colors throughout the painting, as shown in the blue reflective light on the octopus, and soften some edges so they disappear into the background. To finish, punch up the highlights as needed, and add any final details.

Garibaldi in Kelp

This piece is a dramatic study in light effects. The lighting imparts a mysterious quality, and the kelp looks alive and animated. Notice how the brightly colored garibaldi stands out in contrast to the kelp forest.

Before beginning to paint, be sure to plan ahead. In this piece, it is best to paint the ragged edges on the kelp last, rather than trying to paint around them.

After transferring the drawing to the board, use your 1/2" flat brush to cover the surface with a transparent layer of sap green (below). This color is just right for some of the kelp in the background, so instead of painting each leaf, you can just paint the negative areas around some of them. Pat this layer with a soft cloth to remove the brush strokes.

In the second layer (right), using a medium round brush, paint in fairly flat areas of color. Use very dark phthalo green and black for the background kelp, permanent green for the middle ground kelp, and a bright transparent phthalo yellow-green for the foreground kelp. Add green-gold hue or white to the kelp for the lighter areas.

Then paint the fish with a cool alizarin crimson mixed with white, and add a small amount of green-gold hue on its underbelly (left). By adding greens to the fish and some reds to the kelp, the painting becomes more integrated, and the elements look less like cookie-cutter shapes. For the water, mix a little cerulean blue with a lot of white to create an opaque light blue.

Finally, continue to build the layers, deepening the darks with glazes of sap green and bringing up the lights with increasingly opaque colors. Add cadmium red light and cadmium orange to the fish with a pointed fine brush, allowing some of the base color to show through. Graduate the color from orange in the light areas toward red and then to alizarin crimson in the shadows to create volume. To suggest the texture and

patterns of the scales, use small, short strokes with a small flat or round brush, following the curves of the garibaldi's body. Using a fine round brush and a drybrush technique, paint the lighting and texture on the foreground kelp with phthalo yellow-green, cadmium yellow light, and white. Then blend the colors with a dry, soft brush.

Transparent Jellyfish

Jellyfish have a very graceful and elegant movement, and their coloring makes them seem almost surreal. Try to capture these qualities with creative cropping and an imaginative viewing angle. See if you can make this composition "dance."

Keep your paint layers very thin. This painting will be completed almost exclusively with glazes and very little opaque paint.

To define the edges of the jellyfish (above), paint the negative space (background) around them with a fine detail brush. Use layers of very transparent deep phthalo blue glazes that graduate to a cooler ultramarine blue toward the bottom of the painting.

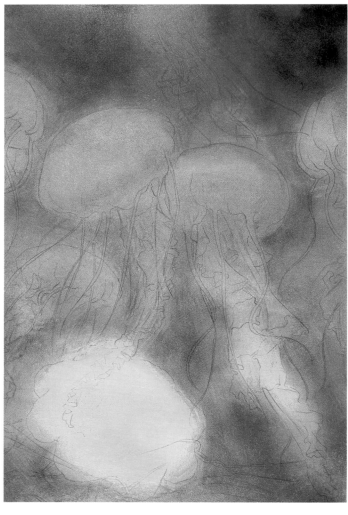

After transferring your drawing to the board, begin to apply the underpainting thinly enough to let the drawing show through.

These are very colorful jellyfish, so glaze them with a variety of colors, such as phthalo blue, magenta, sap green, and alizarin crimson (above). Then soften all the brush strokes with a dry, soft brush.

To show that they recede, make the tendrils increasingly darker as they float into the shadows.

If the jellyfish lack vibrancy, add more intensely colored glazes (above). Then start to define the folds in the tails using semitransparent colors, achieved by mixing white and generous amounts of painting medium. Add warm cadmium reds and cool alizarin crimson with white to the tendrils.

After deepening and defining the background glaze one more time, build up the light areas with a semitransparent glaze of zinc white mixed with a very small amount of cerulean blue. This will create a "milky" effect. Follow your references closely to replicate the outer skin of the jellyfish. They should look both translucent and delicate.

Seals & Sea Lions

This composition shows the scene from both above and below the surface of the water. Viewing the seals from below makes a dramatic composition and creates an excellent study in perspective.

Emphasize the difference between the areas above and below the surface by using warm, bright, and light colors above, and keeping all those below very cool.

To start building up the water, lay in patches of opaque color on top of the underpainting, graduating from phthalo green with white at the surface, to phthalo blue with white in the middle, to ultramarine blue with white at the bottom. Then blend these colors with a dry, soft brush (above).

The sky is farther away than the water is, so the sky should be painted in a cooler tone.

Use a transparent dark sap green to define the leaves of the kelp and to darken the shadow areas on the sea lions underwater.

Use an ultramarine blue glaze for the underpainting of the sky (above). To show the depth in the water, start with a phthalo green glaze at the top, and gradually blend in a phthalo blue glaze until it is the dominant color at the bottom of the painting.

For the sea lions above the water, use warm colors in the light areas and darker glazes for the shadows (above). Paint the buoy with cadmium red light graduating into cool magenta and alizarin crimson with touches of white. Carry these colors to the buoy's underside to distinguish it from the water.

The last step is to paint the final lighting and details. Use a very fine round brush to paint the fur and the details of the seals, including their whiskers.

Then punch up the light where it strikes the sea lions under the water with phthalo green and a lot of white.

Tide Pool

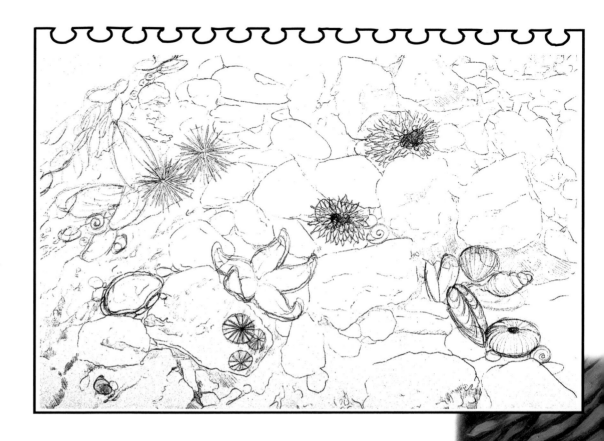

Tide pools are teeming with a wide variety of plants and sea creatures. This composition zooms in close and focuses on a few things in great detail, rather than trying to depict a great number of things more broadly. Notice how each color can be found everywhere in varying amounts. This weaving of color throughout the painting makes it more lively and visually exciting.

The underpainting is done with pale glazes of ultramarine blue on the shadowed side and sap green on the sunlit side. After applying an even, transparent glaze, remove some areas of paint with a soft cloth to create areas of light and shadow and to build volume. Then paint in deeper glazes of phthalo blue and sap green in the shadow areas (below).

Notice how adding deeper glazes dramatically enhances the painting's sense of volume.

For the light surfaces of the stones, use a combination of cadmium orange, yellow ochre, and green-gold hue mixed with white (right). Choose bluish and purplish grays for the areas in shadow. Mix a warm red (cadmium) with a cool blue (ultramarine) to make a reddish purple; mix a cool red (alizarin crimson) with a cool blue for a cooler, bluer purple. To gray the colors, add yellow ochre or burnt umber (and white, if it's too dark).

Add volume by applying drybrushed highlights and details to the shadowed areas of the stones and shells with yellow ochre, cadmium red light with white, and phthalo blue with white (right). Keep the edges above the water crisp and detailed, and soften or blur those below the water.

To illustrate light reflecting on the stones underwater, add subtle patterns of white lines curving over the surface of the stones. Then blend with a soft brush.

Arctic Scene

It's a little more challenging to achieve logical space when you have a lot of subjects in one composition. Sometimes it's helpful to make drawings of the separate parts, and then cut and paste them together in many different combinations until you find one you like. This composition stresses a clear sense of foreground and background, and it uses a circular design to create movement.

Now paint the rocks and seals with cool gray mixes of alizarin crimson and phthalo blue (above). Use black with cobalt blue for the penguins' coats, and start adding some burnt sienna and burnt umber to the bodies of the sea lions. Apply layers of magenta glaze over the shadows to further deepen and cool them. Use white mixed with cadmium yellow light to show where the light strikes the penguins' bellies. Mix green-gold hue with ivory black for the highlights on their dark coats.

Apply an underpainting of ultramarine blue glaze to your drawing. Before the underpainting dries, remove some areas with a soft cloth, and smooth out the gradations of color with a fan brush.

Add additional layers of glaze to the water to show movement on the waves. Refer to the discussion of water effects on page 7.

Finally, fine-tune the details and heighten the colors on the rocks and the backs of the sea lions with gradations of yellow ochre and cadmium red light to burnt sienna and burnt umber with magenta. Use warm whites for the light areas of the iceberg; then punch up the whites on the horizon line and where the water splashes up.

Tropical Reef

This drawing was created by referring to a myriad of reference pictures, from fish and turtles to coral and lighting. In tropical areas, the light comes through shallow water so cleanly and strongly that the colors are very bright and true. The colors seem to dance as they are reflected in the surrounding water and light.

There's a lot going on in this painting, so choose a variety of rich, vibrant colors. Use a combination of glazes, building layer upon layer, to create depth and volume. The strong contrast between light and dark images really brings the painting to life.

For the reef, apply a base glaze of alizarin crimson with a little ultramarine blue.

Use a base of sap green graduating to phthalo blue for the turtle.

Definine the coral with dark glazes of alizarin crimson.

Use bases of cerulean blue and alizarin crimson with white for the small fish.

Establish the puffer fish's volume by graduating from white to a cool purple made with alizarin crimson, phthalo blue, and white.

The most important quality of this painting is its sense of light and atmospheric perspective. Be careful to keep your colors fresh and clean. The background should be very cool, and the fish in the foreground should incorporate a full range of warm and cool colors. Make the forms of the fish crisp and refined, so they come forward visually.

Congratulations! Now you too are an expert at painting sea life, ready to create some masterpieces of your own. Relax, and have fun!

Notice the size relationship between the puffer fish in the foreground and the sea turtle behind the coral. Use variations in size and color to enhance the depth of field.

More Ways to Learn

Artist's Library

The **Artist's Library** series offers both beginning and advanced artists many opportunities to expand their creativity, conquer technical obstacles, and explore new media. You'll find in-depth, thorough information on each subject or art technique featured in the book. Each book is written and illustrated by a well-known artist who is qualified to help take eager learners to a new level of expertise.
Paperback, 64 pages, 6-1/2" x 9-1/2"

Collector's Series

Collector's Series books are excellent additions to any library, offering a comprehensive selection of projects drawn from the most popular titles in our How to Draw and Paint series. These books take the fundamentals of a particular medium, then further explore the subjects, styles, and techniques of featured artists.
CS01, CS02, CS04: Paperback, 144 pages, 9" x 12"
CS03: Paperback, 224 pages, 10-1/4" x 9"

How to Draw and Paint

The **How to Draw and Paint** series includes these five stunning new titles to enhance an extensive collection of books on every subject and medium to meet any artist's needs. Specially written to encourage and motivate, these new books offer essential information in an easy-to-follow format. Lavishly illustrated with beautiful drawings and gorgeous art, this series both instructs and inspires.

Paperback, 32 pages, 10-1/4" x 13-3/4"

Walter Foster products are available at art and craft stores everywhere. Write or call for a FREE catalog that includes all of Walter Foster's titles. Or visit our website at
www.walterfoster.com

Walter Foster Publishing, Inc. • 23062 La Cadena Drive • Laguna Hills, CA 92653 • (800) 426-009